408

Pebble™ Plus

Bugs, Bugs, Bugs!

Butterflies

by Fran Howard

Consulting Editor: Gail Saunders-Smith, PhD
Consultant: Gary A. Dunn, MS, Director of Education
Young Entomologists' Society Inc.
Lansing, Michigan

Capstone press

Mankato, Minnesota

Pebble Plus is published by Capstone Press,
151 Good Counsel Drive, P.O. Box 669, Mankato, Minnesota 56002.
www.capstonepress.com

1 2 3 4 5 6 10 09 08 07 06 05

Library of Congress Cataloging-in-Publication Data
Howard, Fran, 1953–
    Butterflies / by Fran Howard.
    p. cm.—(Pebble plus: bugs, bugs, bugs!)
    Includes bibliographical references and index.
    ISBN 0-7368-3643-8 (hardcover)
    ISBN 0-7368-5101-1 (paperback)
    1. Butterflies—Juvenile literature. I. Title. II. Series.
QL544.2.H69 2005
595.78'9—dc22   2004011970

Summary: Simple text and photographs describe the physical characteristics of butterflies.

Editorial Credits
Sarah L. Schuette, editor; Linda Clavel, set designer; Kate Opseth, book designer; Kelly Garvin,
    photo researcher; Scott Thoms, photo editor

Photo Credits
Bill Johnson, 14–15, 21
Brand X Pictures/Burke/Triolo, back cover
Bruce Coleman Inc./Gail M. Shumway, 6–7, 9; John Henry Williams, cover
Creatas, 1
Minden Pictures/Michael & Patricia Fogden, 5
Pete Carmichael, 17
Robert McCaw, 10–11
Sally McCrae-Kuyper, 13, 18–19

Note to Parents and Teachers

The Bugs, Bugs, Bugs! set supports national science standards related to the diversity
of life and heredity. This book describes and illustrates butterflies. The images support
early readers in understanding the text. The repetition of words and phrases helps early
readers learn new words. This book also introduces early readers to subject-specific
vocabulary words, which are defined in the Glossary section. Early readers may need
assistance to read some words and to use the Table of Contents, Glossary, Read More,
Internet Sites, and Index sections of the book.

Table of Contents

What Are Butterflies?

Butterflies are insects
with thin bodies
and large wings.

How Butterflies Look

Butterflies have

four colorful wings.

7

Most butterflies are about
the size of a child's fist.

Butterflies have two antennas.
Butterflies use their antennas
to feel and smell.

11

Butterflies have thin legs.

Butterflies taste with

their feet.

What Butterflies Do

Butterflies drink nectar
from flowers.
Butterflies have long mouths
that work like straws.

Butterflies fly from flower to flower. Pollen from the flowers sometimes sticks to their legs.

The pollen falls off
when butterflies land
on new flowers.

The pollen helps
new flowers grow.
More butterflies bring
more flowers.

Glossary

antenna—a feeler; insects use antennas to sense movement, to smell, and to listen to each other.

insect—a small animal with a hard outer shell, six legs, three body sections, and two antennas; most insects have wings.

nectar—a sweet liquid found in flowers

pollen—the tiny, yellow grains in flowers; pollen helps plants produce seeds.

Read More

Berger, Melvin, and Gilda Berger. *Butterflies.* Time-to-Discover. New York: Scholastic, 2002.

Hibbert, Clare. *The Life of a Butterfly.* Life Cycles. Chicago: Raintree, 2005.

Watts, Barrie. *Butterfly.* Watch It Grow. North Mankato, Minn.: Smart Apple Media, 2003.

Internet Sites

FactHound offers a safe, fun way to find Internet sites related to this book. All of the sites on FactHound have been researched by our staff.

Here's how:

1. Visit *www.facthound.com*

2. Type in this special code **0736836438** for age-appropriate sites. Or enter a search word related to this book for a more general search.

3. Click on the **Fetch It** button.

FactHound will fetch the best sites for you!

Index

Word Count: 94
Grade: 1
Early-Intervention Level: 10